FRANCIS FRITH'S
TOWN&CITY
MEMORIES

DORKING

JUNE M SPONG was born in Lyminster, Sussex. She moved to Dorking in 1957. She is married with two grown-up children and became interested in family and local history about twenty-five years ago. She was a member of staff for Surrey County Council for twenty years and worked in Dorking Library from 1989. She previously worked for the Mobile Library serving the local villages, where she gleaned much of her knowledge. June retired in February 2005

COLDHARBOUR LANE 1907 57647

FRANCIS FRITH'S

TOWN & CITY

MEMORIES

DORKING

JUNE M SPONG

FRANCIS FRITH'S
TOWN & CITY
MEMORIES

First published as Dorking, A Photographic History of your Town in 2001
by Black Horse Books, an imprint of The Francis Frith Collection.
Revised edition published in the United Kingdom in 2005 by
The Francis Frith Collection as Dorking, Town and City Memories.

Limited Hardback Edition 2005
ISBN 1-84589-017-5
Paperback Edition 2005
ISBN 1-85937-960-5

British Library Cataloguing in Publication Data

Dorking
Town and City Memories
June M Spong

The Francis Frith Collection
Frith's Barn, Teffont,
Salisbury, Wiltshire SP3 5QP
Tel: +44 (0) 1722 716 376
Email: info@francisfrith.co.uk
www.francisfrith.co.uk

Aerial photographs reproduced under licence from Simmons Aerofilms Limited
Historical Ordnance Survey maps reproduced under licence from Homecheck.co.uk
Every attempt has been made to contact copyright holders of illustrative material. We will
be happy to give full acknowledgement in future editions for any items not credited. Any
information should be directed to The Francis Frith Collection.

Printed and bound in England

Front Cover: **DORKING, HIGH STREET 1927** 79499t
The colour-tinting in this image is for illustrative purposes only,
and is not intended to be historically accurate

FRANCIS FRITH'S
TOWN & CITY
MEMORIES

CONTENTS

F rancis Frith, Victorian founder of the world-famous photographic archive, was a devout Quaker and a highly successful Victorian businessman. By 1860 he was already a multi-millionaire, having established and sold a wholesale grocery business in Liverpool. He had also made a series of pioneering photographic journeys to the Nile region. The images he returned with were the talk of London. An eminent modern historian has likened their impact on the population of the time to that on our own generation of the first photographs taken on the surface of the moon.

Frith had a passion for landscape, and was as equally inspired by the countryside of Britain as he was by the desert regions of the Nile. He resolved to set out on a new career and to use his skills with a camera. He established a business in Reigate as a specialist publisher of topographical photographs.

Frith lived in an era of immense and sometimes violent change. For the poor in the early part of Victoria's reign work was a drudge and the hours long, and ordinary people had precious little free time. Most had not travelled far beyond the boundaries of their own town or village. Mass tourism was in its infancy during the 1860s, but during the next decade the railway network and the establishment of Bank Holidays and half-Saturdays gradually made it possible for the working man and his family to enjoy holidays and to see a little more of the world. With characteristic business acumen, Francis Frith foresaw that these new tourists would enjoy having souvenirs to commemorate their days out. He began selling photo-souvenirs of seaside resorts and beauty spots, which the Victorian public pasted into treasured family albums.

Frith's aim was to photograph every town and village in Britain. For the next thirty years he travelled the country by train and by pony and trap, producing fine photographs of seaside resorts and beauty spots that were keenly bought by millions of Victorians.

THE RISE OF FRITH & CO

Each photograph was taken with tourism in mind, the small team of Frith photographers concentrating on busy shopping streets, beaches, seafronts, picturesque lanes and villages. They also photographed buildings: the Victorian and Edwardian eras were times of huge building activity, and town halls, libraries, post offices, schools and technical colleges were springing up all over the country. They were invariably celebrated by a proud Victorian public, and photo souvenirs – visual records – published by F Frith & Co were sold in their hundreds of thousands. In addition, many new commercial buildings such as hotels, inns and pubs were photographed, often because their owners specifically commissioned Frith postcards or prints of them for re-sale or for publicity purposes.

In order to gain some understanding of the scale of Frith's business one only has to look at the catalogue issued by Frith & Co in 1886: it runs to some 670 pages. By 1890 Frith had created the greatest specialist photographic publishing company in the world, with over 2,000 stockists! The picture on the right shows the Frith & Co display board on the wall of the stockist at Ingleton in the Yorkshire Dales (left of window). Beautifully constructed with a mahogany frame and gilt inserts, it displayed a dozen scenes.

POSTCARD BONANZA

The ever-popular holiday postcard we know today took many years to appear, and F Frith & Co was in the vanguard of its development. Postcards became a hugely popular means of communication and sold in their millions. Frith's company took full advantage of this boom and soon became the major publisher of photographic view postcards.

Francis Frith died in 1898 at his villa in Cannes, his great project still growing. His sons Eustace and Cyril continued their father's monumental task, expanding the number of views offered to the public and recording more and more places in Britain, as the coasts and countryside were opened up to mass travel. The archive Frith created continued in business for another seventy years. By 1970 it contained over a third of a million pictures of 7,000 cities, towns and villages. The massive photographic record Frith has left to us stands as a living monument to a special and very remarkable man.

This book shows your town as it was photographed by this world-famous archive at various periods in its development over the past 150 years. Every photograph was taken for a specific commercial purpose, which explains why the selection may not show every aspect of the town landscape. However, the photographs, compiled from one of the world's most celebrated archives, provide an important and absorbing record of your town.

DORKING FROM THE AIR 1921 AF6291

INTRODUCTION

Dorking is one of the many historical towns in the county of Surrey. In the Domesday Book of 1086, it has a Saxon name, Dorchinges. The name itself probably means 'the people of Deorc', and may refer to the name of the first settler; the last syllable 'ingas' is a typical Saxon place-name suffix, which possibly dates the settlement from the 7th or 8th centuries AD. On her travels, Celia Fiennes referred to the town as Darken. This spelling was probably due to the local accent she heard. In Brabner's Gazetteer (1895) we read that 'the most probable derivation of the word Dorking is from the Celtic Darach, an oak'.

The town is situated 25 miles south-west from the city of London. It lies on the cross-roads of the A24 London to Worthing road and the A25 Maidstone to Guildford road; it sits in the shadow of Box Hill, in the valley of the River Mole. The Dorking area boasts some of the finest scenery in Surrey, including Box Hill, Leith Hill, Betchworth, Abinger, Friday Street, Wotten and Ranmore, and all of these can be seen from the summit of the hill. Dorking's boundary parishes to the north are Mickleham and Great Bookham; on the east are Betchworth and Brockham; to the south lie Newdigate, Leigh, Capel and Ockley; and to the west are Westcott and Wotten. Dorking is twelve miles from both Guildford and Horsham, five

from Leatherhead and about nine from Redhill.

Dorking stands on one of the ancient trackways, one of the four 'Royal Roads'. The road crossed the north-west corner of the churchyard and passed through the town. The Romans visited Dorking, and there is evidence of a settlement here. (The Roman occupation of Britain was approximately from the 1st to the 4th centuries AD). A military road, later called Stane Street, was constructed in the first century AD for the purpose of carrying supplies to and from London and Chichester. Remains of Stane Street can be seen towards Ockley, where many Saxon arrowheads and coins have been found. There was also another settlement on one of the high parts of the town of Dorking — Roman coins were found in the churchyard. There is a circular, double-ditched camp at Anstibury, just west of the village of Holmwood. There was also a camp and villa at Ashtead, where bricks were made; these were carted along Stane Street to Verulamium (St Albans). At the bottom of Box Hill, Stane Street crossed the Mole at the Burford Bridge and the Dorking Gap. During the excavation of pits and ditches, several finds were made of jewellery, pottery, and tiles. Examples of these can be seen on show in Robert Dyas in the High Street, and at the Dorking Museum.

Dorking has four remaining mills. Castle Mill sits by the River Mole beside Reigate Road. It closed in 1942, and is now a private residence; it is open on Heritage Days once a year. Pixham Mill is in the suburb of Pixham, and closed in 1910. Pippbrook Mill closed in 1932, and a publisher of children's books now occupies it. Attlee's Old Parsonage Mill was demolished in 1959, but grain continues to be processed in the new buildings by the original owners.

A stream called the Pip Brook runs parallel with the town on its north side, which runs into the River Mole at Box Hill. In times past, the streams in the neighbourhood were famous for producing perch; these were much liked by Dutch merchants, who came frequently from London to sample water-souchy soup, a local delicacy.

The town stands on the Greensand Way. There are extensive cave workings under the streets of Dorking, which were once privately-owned and used for storage by the High Street shops. Now only a few can be viewed on special open days.

The population of Dorking is now approximately 10,600. Its population in 1931 was 8,058, and in 1911 it was 7,700. If we include the surrounding villages, the present population would exceed 20,000. There are three main streets, two Anglican Churches, one Catholic Church and six places of worship for other denominations. There are nineteen public houses (there were as many as thirty-six up until the middle of the 1960s), three hotels and plenty of restaurants and snack bars. There is also a sports centre, two libraries, the offices of the Mole Valley District Council, two supermarkets, thirteen hairdressing salons, three florists, four banks, nine estate agents and three outlet garages. Dorking has a weekly market and a monthly farmers' market, and for entertainment it has the Dorking Halls.

Our tour of Dorking goes from north to south.

THE DORKING AREA 1910 (GEOGRAPHIA RAMBLERS'
GUIDE TO DORKING NO.1 C1920)

CASTLE MILL 1909 61414

THE NORTHERN PARISHES

When travelling south from Leatherhead, we pass on our right the fine house in Norbury Park; it is said to be one of the loveliest estates in Surrey. Preserved by Surrey County Council, it is most famous for its ancient yews. It was home to William Locke (1863-1930), born in Barbados, novelist, dramatist and architect. He 'spared no expense to make it beautiful', and later sold it to Dr Marie Stopes, the pioneer of birth control.

To our left is the entrance to the Old London Road, which leads to Mickleham, one of Dorking's neighbouring parishes. The village boasts many grand buildings. Box Hill School has become one of the dominant features of the village; it was erected by Edward Gardener in 1870, and was then named Dalewood. The Army requisitioned the building as headquarters for the Pay Corps during World War II. After the war, it became St Nicholas's school. In 1959 a housemaster from Gordonstoun founded what is now Box Hill School, which accommodates approximately 300 boys and girls, both boarding and day pupils.

JUNIPER HALL

Just a few hundred yards to the right of the village is Juniper Hall. Stane Street passes close by to the west of the house. The first known building on the site was an alehouse named the Royal Oak, which probably originated in the 17th century. Sir Cecil Bishop acquired the property in the late 18th century; he died in 1779, after extending the property and converting it into a family residence. Lady Templeton, the wife of an Irish peer, worked closely with the Wedgwoods to create the Templeton Room, which is in the style of Robert Adam. Then Mr David Jenkinson, a wealthy lottery owner, bought the hall. It was he who built Juniper Hill whilst living in Juniper Hall, and he also commissioned Benjamin Elliott to plant the cedars of Lebanon. Jenkinson, who was living in Juniper Hill during 1792-3, let the Hall; it became a refuge to French aristocrats

who were fleeing their homeland during the Revolution. The band of exiles was led by Madame de Brogue; among them were the Marquis de Lafayette, Madame de Stael and Monsieur d'Arblay, who later married Frances (Fanny) Burney, one of Dorking's most famous authors, in Mickleham Church in 1793. Fanny Burney is well-known for 'Evalina' and other novels, and for her diary. After their marriage they lived in Westhumble, where Fanny continued to write.

Juniper Hall was bought by a wealthy landowner, Jonathon Worrell, who had estates in Barbados and Prince Edward Island. On his death in 1800 the Hall became the home of Thomas Broadwood the piano maker, who bought it from Mrs Worrell for the sum of £8,236 10s. The Hall had three more owners up to the beginning of the Second World War; it was then occupied by a Canadian military base that practically destroyed the interior by burning the wall panelling to keep warm. The last owner, Miss McAndrew, sold the property to the National Trust in 1945 as part of the Trust's Box Hill Estate. It was leased in 1946 to the Council for Promotion of Field Studies, and is open to students of all ages. It has been run by the Field Studies Council since 1956.

BOX HILL

Box Hill takes its name from the many box trees which grow there. In 1797, Thomas Howard, Earl of Arundel, planted many trees on the hill, which had been sold to him by Sir John Mildway for the sum of £10,000. The box tree (buxus sempervirens), a native of the Mediterranean and China, is mainly used as a garden edging plant in formal gardens. It is an evergreen growing to twenty to thirty feet. Its wood is widely used for tool handles and the manufacture of flutes and clarinets, and it is also used for inlay work with ivory.

Box Hill is one of the natural wonders of Surrey. From the summit there is a spectacular view of the surrounding landscape, including Mickleham Downs, the Dorking Gap, Norbury Park, Ranmore, Betchworth, Brockham, Leigh and the South Downs, and also the

BOX HILL, THE SLOPES C1890 55712B

The Victorians visited for relaxation, to walk up the hill and to admire the view. Before and after the war, thousands came by car, train and charabanc or even by bicycle from London and the suburbs to take in the country air, or to walk along the Mole. Now, each Sunday hundreds of motorcycles congregate at the foot of the hill to show off their machines.

River Mole, so named, it is said, because it disappears beneath the hill into the subterranean clefts in the chalk, only to reappear again near Leatherhead. The disappearance of the river has caused much speculation over the centuries, and it gave rise to many different legends, tales and folklore. Camden wrote of the mystery of the Mole in his 'Britannia' (1610). Box Hill is one of Surrey's most visited beauty spots, and one of the finest views around. The hill rises 400 feet from the river Mole to the summit; it is said to be the grandest piece of natural cliff in southern England.

The Lookout at the summit of Box Hill is due to the generosity of Mr Leopold Salomons of Norbury Park. It was given so that 'the public has the privilege of using the hill to view the southern part of the county, and counties beyond'; it is dedicated to the memory of George Meredith. Mr Salomons bought the land to be held in safe-keeping for the nation, and to save it from urban developers. He kindly presented it to the people to be managed by the National Trust.

Another monument on the hill is a memorial to Major Peter Labelliere, an eccentric resident of Dorking; on 11 July 1800 he was buried upside-down, at his request. He wanted to be buried this way so that 'when the world turns topsy-turvy he would be the right way up'. It is said that he walked the streets like a tramp and never washed. The Major asked in his will that his landlady's daughter 'will dance on my grave'; legend has it that she did not fulfil his request.

Also associated with Dorking and Box Hill was Colonel George Tomkyns Chesney (1830-95). Born into a distinguished military family, he entered the Bengal Lancers as a second lieutenant in 1848. He was recalled to England in 1870, and founded the Royal Indian Civil Engineering College at Staines. In 1871 he sent the outline of a short story to Blackwood's Magazine predicting a national catastrophe. It was published as 'The Battle of Dorking: Reminiscences of a Volunteer', and told the story of an invasion by the French. It alarmed the nation, angered the Prime Minister, and astonished Europe. Although fictitious, it gave a good account of how Britain could be conquered. All the enemy had to do was to land on the coast and march over the Weald, pass through the Dorking Gap, and then march on to London and victory. Chesney had written from military experience; his writing did not go unnoticed, and steps were taken to stem any invasion in the future. Conan Doyle, author of the Sherlock Holmes stories, was a fan of 'The Battle of Dorking', and in a novel of the same name, Glen Petrie continued the tales of Mycroft Holmes, the elder brother of Sherlock.

THE BURFORD BRIDGE HOTEL

Dorking's most prominent feature is St Martin's Church, which can be seen from the four points of the compass when entering the town; and the most appealing feature as we approach Dorking on the A24 is the Burford Bridge Hotel, which nestles beneath the slopes of Box Hill. It is thought that the first building on this site was built as early as 1629; it was then known as Cockscroft, and had barns and an orchard. By 1792 James Charman owned the property, which became known as the Fox and Hounds. James's son William developed it into a substantial property, basically the one we see today. Lord Nelson made frequent visits, and it has been said that he met Lady Hamilton here on the eve of the Battle of Trafalgar, and that they frequently courted here. There is now a room named after Lady Hamilton, and their pictures adorn the walls. In 1801 Nelson wrote in his diary: 'What a pretty place, and we were all so happy'.

BOX HILL, THE ZIGZAG C1955 D45051

Just a short journey beyond Juniper Hall, we pass the Zigzag: this is the western approach to the summit of Box Hill. It is only a hundred yards or so to the beginning of the struggle up a chalk path, and a steep climb to the summit. There is another road leading to the hill just north of the village of Betchworth. The railway station at Betchworth had its beginnings transporting the lime from Betchworth lime kilns during the 19th and early 20th centuries.

Above: THE BURFORD BRIDGE HOTEL 1900 55718A

Far Left: THE BURFORD BRIDGE HOTEL 1897 38995

Centre: THE BURFORD BRIDGE HOTEL 1922 71814

Left: THE BURFORD BRIDGE HOTEL C1965 D45101

An old coaching inn, the Hotel stands on land once owned by
Walter de Merton, founder of Merton College, Oxford. The hotel
has changed little over the last hundred years, and is very popular
venue for weddings and functions.

Top: THE FORT TEA GARDENS C1955 D45088

Above: THE WIMPY BAR (ORIGINALLY THE FORT TEA GARDENS) C1965 D45205

DORKING'S FAMOUS VISITORS

There have been many prominent visitors to Dorking who came to see its beautiful scenery and dwell in its peace and tranquillity. They include Jane Austen, Daniel Defoe, Sheridan, Henry Dendy and Charles Mackay. Artists such as John Beckett, Walter Dendy Sadler (born in Dorking), Abraham Hulk junior, Cornelius Varley and Hassell all came to paint the scenery. Robert Louis Stevenson came, and walked on Box Hill to gain inspiration; he wrote some of 'The New Arabian Nights' here. Other visitors were John Wesley, Sir Walter Scott, Charles Dickens, John Keats, John Evelyn, Samuel Pepys and Celia Fiennes.

Queen Victoria visited her favourite poet and novelist, George Meredith, who for forty years lived in Flint Cottage on the slopes of Box Hill. Other frequent visitors to Flint Cottage were J M Barrie and Henry James. Meredith named Juniper Bottom 'Happy Valley', and instigated the 'Sunday Tramps'; Leslie Stephen, James C Robertson, R L Stevenson, Hilaire Belloc and Carlyle frequently accompanied him. As Meredith grew older he became crippled, but he insisted on continuing his jaunts with the aid of a bath chair, and was taken out every day to view his beloved Box Hill. Meredith wrote in 1882: 'Nowhere in England is there richer foliage, or wilder downs and fresher woodlands'.

It was here that he wrote most of his works; 'Diana of the Crossways' was based on Crossways Farm at Abinger. Meredith is buried in the churchyard on the Reigate Road with his second wife and children.

WESTHUMBLE

This small village lies just to the west at the foot of Box Hill; the nearest railway station to the hill is named 'Box Hill & Westhumble'.

Just past the Stepping Stones public house is one of the roads leading to Polesden Lacy. This was once the home of Richard Brinsley Sheridan, who purchased the property, then known as High Polesden, in 1796. The estate dates to the early 13th century, and was owned by William de Polesdene. It was later occupied by Thomas Slyfield, and was granted to John Norbury in 1470. Sir Thomas Cubitt built the present house in the early 1820s. Edward VII frequented Polesden Lacy so that he could enjoy peace and solitude with his friends and retreat from the hustle and bustle of London, thanks to the hospitality of the Hon Captain and Mrs Grevill. George VI, then Duke of York, honeymooned here with Elizabeth Bowes Lyon, later the Queen Mother. On Mrs Grevill's death in 1942, the estate was willed to the National Trust and became their Southern Area Office.

General Sir E Hamley was another who was afraid of an imminent invasion. His was the thought behind the fortresses that were built in the late 1880s on and around Box Hill; there is still a fort on the summit of the hill, a testimony of a war that was never fought. Hamley started a campaign to build the fortresses in case of an invasion from France, and lobbied parliament until they agreed to his venture. Volunteers were to be enlisted to build and man the forts that would be positioned around London. The Government approved Hamley's idea in 1888, and gave permission for the forts to be built.

Just a short distance from the Burford Bridge Hotel is Burford Lodge. At one time it was a private house; then it became offices and workshops for the South Eastern Electricity Board, and is now flats.

PIXHAM

Soon we approach a roundabout. To the left is the hamlet of Pixham, a suburb of Dorking.

It boasts a Lutyens church, which was built in 1903. The school is also a prominent feature: it was designed by the architect Gilbert Redgrave, and opened in July 1880 with twenty-seven pupils. It is here that we find Pixham Mill, now a private residence.

Left:
The Stepping Stones 1932 85408

On our left as we approach Dorking from the north are the Stepping Stones. Contrary to belief, the much-photographed Stepping Stones are not that old. They were originally put into position in 1932, but by 1946 they had deteriorated; they were replaced at the expense of James Chuter Ede, then Home Secretary, who had spent his schooldays in the area, and had many links with Surrey. Clement Attlee, then Prime Minister, who had family connections with Dorking, opened the new stones — Mr Attlee's brother is buried in Dorking Cemetery. A short distance downstream is an iron footbridge, built as a memorial to members of the Ramblers Association who lost their lives in the two World Wars.

Below Left:
Pixham Mill 1931 84182

Below Right:
Burford Lodge 1909 61417

DENBIES ESTATE

To the right of the roundabout is the entrance to Denbies Estate, England's largest family-owned vineyard. On the top of Ashcombe Hill (now Ranmore Hill) there was a farm; here, perhaps, John Denby lived, a one-time farmer who was referred to at a Court Baron held in 1555. A later owner was a Mr Wakeford who, in 1754, sold the property to Jonathan Tyre, the founder of Vauxhall Gardens. Tyre transformed the farm buildings into a modest Georgian house, which was given the name of Denbies. When Tyre died in 1767, the Hon Peter King purchased the estate. On his death his son, Lord King, sold the property to James White; in 1787 he then sold it to Joseph Denison, a London merchant banker. Denison died in 1806, leaving the estate to his son, William Joseph Denison, who became a Member of Parliament for West Surrey in 1818. The estate was greatly enlarged by further purchases of land, from which he created extensive gardens. It later passed to his daughter Elizabeth, whose son was Lord Albert Conyngham. He was later created Lord Londesborough.

Thomas Cubitt purchased Denbies in the autumn of 1850; he had come to Dorking and Ranmore at the height of his very successful building career. He had developed Belgravia, designed Osborne House on the Isle of Wight for Queen Victoria, and built the east front of Buckingham Palace. He also helped Prince Albert with the Great Exhibition of 1851. He set about improving the estate by planting thousands of shrubs and trees and modernising the farm and buildings. He soon demolished the old house, and on higher ground to the south built a palace in the style of Osborne and Belgravia. It was built of brick and stucco with flat Italianate details, and had a Portland stone balustrade round the first floor and roof.

Cubitt built every modern facility into the house, including the insulation of the ceilings with snail and other shells, and he also improved access to the estate — he had his own railway siding, as well as three entrance drives. Unfortunately, he did not live long to enjoy his masterpiece; he died in December 1855. His son, George, who married Laura Joyce, daughter of the vicar of Dorking, inherited the estate and continued his father's improvements. Prince Albert was invited to Denbies on its completion. The estate eventually gave employment to 400 people. In 1892 George became the first Lord Ashcombe and a Member of Parliament for West Surrey. The house was demolished in 1953. The estate buildings are all now part of Denbies Winery, with a reception centre, a restaurant, conference rooms and a gift shop. The Winery also houses the Performing Arts Library, which holds the Ralph Vaughan Williams Collection and the music and arts library for Surrey. Cubitt's statue now stands at the entrance to Reigate Road by the Mole Valley District Council Offices.

Above Right:
DENBIES MANSION 1905 53335A

Below: Right
BOXHILL
(NOW CALLED DEEPDENE) STATION 1907 57652

Deepdene Avenue 1906 54672

Continuing along southwards we pass the Friends Provident Life Office building on the left. We then cross the main-line railway, the second of our railway stations. Opposite is Ashcombe Road and Ashcombe School. A little further on we pass Deepdene Station (once called Boxhill) to our left (illustrated on page 25). To the right is the old London Road. A short distance further on is the junction of the A25 and A24. Deepdene Avenue looks very different now to the way it did at the beginning of the 20th century. The children in photograph 54672 (pages 26-27) are on about the same spot as the garage in photograph D45227 (below).

DEEPDENE AVENUE (THE A24) C1965 D45227

REIGATE ROAD 1906 55701

CHARLES ROSE, 'RECOLLECTIONS OF OLD DORKING', 1876-1877

'A walk through the streets on a summer's day half-a-century ago ... was different in many respects. Let us first, however, get a glimpse of the old town by an imaginary walk through its streets. We enter at a place by London Road, say on a summer's morning ... Although yet early, the mill by the roadside is already at work, and the forge of the blacksmith's shop at the Reigate Road corner is in full blast. We pass along by the southern entrance of the neighbouring nursery grounds ... The chestnut trees hard by the broad green meadow, the mill-pond, and the distant hill are each of them objects of beauty.'

REIGATE ROAD

Dorking has a large cemetery just to the edge of the town on the Reigate Road (see 55702 pages 30-31). At a rough count over 10,000 souls have been buried here since its opening in 21 November 1855. The cemetery buildings are open to view on Heritage Days in September each year. They consist of the main chapel, which is in permanent use. Also on view is the redundant Nonconformist chapel and the mortuary.

A cemetery trail provides a guide to the many notables buried here. They include a VC, Lance Corporal Charles Graham Robertson, 10th Battalion the Royal Fusiliers; the date of Gazette was 9 April 1918, and he died in Dorking on 10 May 1954. He also received the Military Medal.

Also in the cemetery are the Shearburn and Stillwell family vaults, and the Bentall plot — the Bentall family started the famous department store in Kingston. Lying side-by-side are Miss Edith Mary Corderoy and Mr Thomas E Powell, who together started the Dorking British School (now the Powell Corderoy School) in the late 1890s. Also here is Richard Burberry, a member of the famous Burberry raincoat family. Noteable people already mentioned are George Meredith and his family, the Attlee family and General Sir Arthur Cotton DMC. Another fine artist buried here is William (Bill) Brunel, a photographer who was noted for his fine pictures of motor car racing. Also in the churchyard are some fine specimens of trees, including a western red cedar, a deodar cedar and a monkey puzzle tree.

Facing the cemetery is the Happy Eater roadhouse. The motel was built in 1971 in the form of a two-story building; it has 29 bedrooms, which have splendid views of Box Hill. The main building was once one of the many pubs in Dorking. Its original name was the Punch Bowl Inn; it was built in 1780 and designed by Sir John Soane (1753-1837), the distinguished architect and collector of Greek and Roman artefacts. The inn was situated on the edge of the Deepdene estate, and was well known for its beer-garden. James Graves held the licence in 1891. The area was the site of the Punchbowl Fairs.

Also on the Reigate Road are the Watermill Restaurant (see D45110, page 32) and Boxhill Farm.

At the cross-roads is the entrance to the town. On the right is the Mole Valley Council Offices, opened in 1984; the building is not in keeping with the character of the town, but architecturally it is a good design. Opposite is the Dorking Halls, designed by Percy W Meredith in Art Deco style and opened in January 1931 (see 87292 opposite). There is a bronze tablet in the entrance hall to the memory of Ralph Vaughan Williams OM (1872-1958) and at the entrance stands a bronze statue of the composer whitch was errected in April 2001. The Leith Hill Musical Festival was founded in 1905 by Lady Margaret Farrer of Abinger Hall, Vaughan Williams's sister.

REIGATE ROAD

THE CEMETERY 1906 55702

THE WATERMILL RESTAURANT
c1965 D45110

THE PUNCH BOWL INN 1907
57651

PIPPBROOK HOUSE

In the grounds behind the Council Offices stands Pippbrook House, the home of Dorking's main Library. It was once a private house. One of the first known owners of the property was a member of the Brocke family by the name of Ayre. The earliest boundary was north of the stream known now as the Pip Brook. The owner of the lands was Walter atte Pyppe with his wife Aloucia. It was in the 37th year of the reign of Henry VIII that the property passed into the possession of William Burt; no heir could be found after his death, so the Manorial Courts passed the property to his cousin Elizabeth, who had married William Ap. By 1650, the estate had been broken up into six to seven parts of varying sizes, with the main estate being known as Pippbrook. In 1758 William Page pulled down the existing

house for a new building; he remained the owner and occupier for approximately five years. Mr Mark Basket later occupied it. An unknown artist painted it as it was in 1770: the house can be seen as it was in the 18th century set in a panoramic view of Dorking. The painting hangs in the Committee Room at Lords cricket ground.

William Crawford purchased Pippbrook in 1817, and made it his country home for some 20 years. William Crawford served his early life with the East India Company and returned with a handsome fortune. He was a partner in the East India Mercantile House of Crawford, Colwin and Company. Politically, he was in favour of the abolition of the Window Taxes and opposed to short Parliaments and the Corn Laws. An unsuccessful candidate for Brighton at the general election in 1832, he was returned for London in August 1833, and sat until he was defeated in June 1841. The property passed to his son William S Crawford, MP for the City of London, and Chairman of the Dorking bench.

William Henry Forman, a wealthy ironmaster from South Wales, bought Pippbrook House in 1856. He almost completely rebuilt the original structure with the help of Sir George Gilbert Scott. This great architect, renowned for his Gothic designs, was also instrumental in the building of Ranmore Church, the Albert Memorial in Hyde Park, the government offices in Whitehall and Glasgow University. Scott re-built and restructured the house as we see it today. The conversion of the 18th-century house into a Gothic mansion was costly, to say the least. No money was spared on the interior and fittings.

On William Forman's death, his brother Thomas resided in Pippbrook with his wife Elizabeth. After she was widowed, Elizabeth Forman married Major Thomas Seymore Burt. She continued to live in Pippbrook with her husband until her death in 1889. (The Forman and Burt coats of arms can be seen in the east window of St Martin's Church). The property became a subject of a family dispute again; it was eventually sold by order of the Court of Chancery in 1891, and was purchased by Mr Thomas Aggs of Clapham Common. Mr Aggs died in 1897 and his widow, Anna Christy Aggs, continued to live at Pippbrook until her death in 1913. Their son, Henry Gurney Aggs, inherited the property.

In 1928 John Alexander Lloyd purchased Pippbrook House. On his death in 1930, it was sold for £39,000 to Dorking Urban District

The Dorking Halls 1936 87292

The halls were financed and built by a private local company in which Howard Martineau, the Duke of Newcastle and Vaughan Willams were involved. The halls were extensively refurbished and reopened in April 1997 at a cost of over two and a half million pounds; there is now a theatre, a bar, a cafeteria and a cinema.

High Street 1927 79499

Left:
HIGH STREET 1937 87851

Below Left:
HIGH STREET C1965 D45169

Below Right:
HIGH STREET C1967 D45239

HIGH STREET

Right:
HIGH STREET 1905 53334

On market days hair cutting was performed at the side of the Market Place just outside the White Horse Inn (the white building, centre right). Teeth were also pulled, probably from the same chair and by the same technician. There was a permanent dentist's surgery in the basement of the Red Lion Hotel.

Below Left:
HIGH STREET 1890 27388

Below Right:
THE POST OFFICE AT THE CORNER OF HIGH AND NORTH STREETS 1900 46018

There was also a prosperous pleasure fair in the early 1800s which sold a variety of goods and amusements for the children. The trades of the Victorian shops were multifarious, and many businesses stayed open from dawn until after dark, sometimes trading as late as nine o'clock in the evenings.

The market moved from the High Street to a new site behind the north side of the High Street in 1926. This was closed as a livestock market in the early 1960s and has been replaced by the new Saint Martin's Walk with shops. There is a market (near to the old site) held in the car park each Friday, and a farmers' market is held here once a month.

During the past centuries football was played in the High Street on Shrove Tuesday. Three balls, one white, one red and one blue, were paraded around the town. The balls were inscribed 'Wind and Water is Dorking's Glory'. The shops closed their shutters and boarded up their windows for fear of broken glass. The red ball was kicked off by the boys at 3 o'clock, and the blue ball by the men, and then at 4 o'clock all the players took up the game with the white ball until the church clock chimed six. Ale was consumed after the game had finished, and money was collected for charity.

The Dorking Fowl is a breed of chicken and takes its name from the town; it was extensively bred here, and was probably brought to England with the Roman invasion. A peculiar characteristic of the breed is that it possesses a fifth claw. It is compact, plump in build, and bred for the breast; it carries more meat in proportion to its size than any other fowl, and in quantity and flavour its flesh is excellent. As a layer, the hen compares favourably with any other birds of its size and weight. It was a favourite on the table of Queen Victoria, who would only eat eggs from the Dorking hen. The cock has silver and black/green plumage. There are three main colour variations: the Red, the Silver Grey and the Dark Dorking. In 'The Countryman', Spring 1975, there appeared a picture of a Silver Grey Dorking Cock: 'The Dorking is regarded as Britain's oldest breed of fowl. Julius Caesar mentioned the existence of a domestic fowl in Britain in 55BC, and the Roman historian Columbella describes a breed much prized for its table-qualities. His description fits closely to the Dorking fowl of recent centuries, including the unusual fifth toe ...'

Above:
HIGH STREET 1922 71736

Right :
HIGH STREET C1965 D45155

Meadowbank 1905 53332A

THE MILL POND 1906 54669

Relaxation from the busy streets could be found near the High Street at Meadowbank and at the Mill Pond.

INNS AND PUBLIC HOUSES

There were many public houses and inns in the town. Those still trading are the Surrey Yeoman (see 46016 overleaf), the Bull's Head (Rose Hill, which we can see in 54666, right, with its entrance on the corner of the High Street and just behind the Bull's Head), the White Hart, the Jolly Butchers, the Malthouse (formerly the Rising Sun), the Spotted Dog, the Cricketers Arms, the Queen's Head, the Pilgrim (formerly the Station Hotel), the Bush, the Windmill (now closed), the Stepping Stones, the Royal Oak, the Plough, the Falkland Arms, the Prince of Wales, the Star and the Old House at Home. The King's Arms, in West Street, opened as a coaching inn by Edward Goodwyn in about 1590 to catch the Guildford to London trade.

Those that are no longer trading are the Ram, the Three Tonnes, the Market House, the Grapes, the Sun, the Wheatsheaf (now a bookshop), the Chequers Arms, the Bricklayers Arms, the Gun (the building remains), the Old King's Arms, the White Lion, the Arundel Arms (now housing), the Queen's Arms, the Rose & Crown (a lighting shop), the Bell (solicitors), the Pig & Piece of Pink String and the Beehive (now a private house). The rest have been demolished. The Red Lion, which was demolished in 1964, was a hotel, as is the White Horse, which sits in the centre of the town, and the Lincoln Arms, which stands in Lincoln Road at the entrance to the main line railway station; it was originally called the Star and Garter.

Brewers and maltsters became established in the town during the 19th and 20th centuries: Griffen Beal of Westcott, John Young (1897) in West Street, and William Boxall who owned the Sun Brewery in the High Street. Boxall's was taken over by the Swan Brewery of Leatherhead in April 1907. Edward Lucock was also in the High Street, and James Cheeseman had his brewery in South Street. The Red Lion Brewery was also in the High Street. A large quantity of ale must have been consumed during business hours and on market days. The Spotted Dog was originally opened as a beer shop soon after the Duke of Wellington Beer Act.

A R HOPE MONCRIEFF, 'SURREY', 1934

'Its [Dorking's] importance in the good old days is vouched for by the size and number of its inns; the White Horse and the Red Lion are still flourishing ... The curious stranger searches in vain for the sign of the Marquis of Granby, for the tomb of Mrs Sam Weller, senior, or for the chapel at which Mr Stiggins ministered ...'

ROSE HILL 1906 54666

Above Left:
THE WHITE HORSE HOTEL c1960   D45072

This is said to be the oldest inn in the town. Charles Dickens is reputed to have penned 'The Pickwick Papers' on one of his many visits to Dorking. The inn has changed little in its appearance over the last two centuries. A glass of ale can still be comfortably supped in front of the log fire, and the oak beams and carved staircase stand as they did in Dickens's time. A pleasant hour or two can still be spent in the cobbled courtyard on a sunny day. The inn enhances one of the most pleasant-looking town centres in the area. It stands on the old Stane Street, and has been known as a resting-place for travellers for perhaps nearly a thousand years. Early evidence of a building on this site dates from 1278. Some of the earliest parts of the old building can still be found under the foundations of the present site.

Below Left:
THE SURREY YEOMAN, HIGH STREET 1900   46016

L COLLISON MORLEY
'COMPANION INTO SURREY', 1938

'The one desire of every true Briton on first coming to Dorking is to follow Sam Weller as he descends from the Arundel coach to the Marquis of Granby. The Marquis, it is true, had no more life outside Dickens's brain than Sam himself, but its counterpart in our everyday world is said to have lain in North Street, the King's Head, a vast establishment in the 18th century, now vanished, like the Post Office that succeeded it'.

CHURCHES AND MEETING HOUSES

St Martin's Church stands just off the High Street. It was rebuilt in the late 19th century, and its spire stands 210ft high. Large and handsome, it boasts two fine stained glass windows depicting the coats of arms of the Burt and Forman families of Pippbrook House. The Formans took an active part in Dorking life, and were noted for founding the existing church.

The old church of St Martin's dominated the skyline prior to 1869; it stood on an existing religious site believed to be on the Pilgrims' Way — Domesday records show a religious site on this spot. Rebuilt twice during the second half of the 19th century, the present church was constructed between 1869 and 1877. The Right Rev Samuel Wilberforce, Bishop of Winchester, laid the foundation stone, and the tower was built in 1873. The bells were hung in 1877, but were removed in March 1998 to allow repair work to be carried out on the bell tower. The new bells were hung in April 1998 and first pealed out on 19 May that year.

The Rev Henry Joyce, born in 1817, curate of St Martin's, was educated at Charterhouse and Oxford, and ordained in 1842. William, his son, was curate here, and then succeeded his father to the living of St Martin's in 1850. For as long as thirty years the Joyce family served St Martin's. After William his brother, the Rev John Wayland Joyce served as curate to his father. Later his nephew, the Rev James Barclay Joyce, son of William Wayland Joyce, also served as curate from 1875 to 1876.

CHURCHES AND MEETING HOUSES

Left:

SOUTH STREET AND THE WESLEYAN CHURCH c1955 D45008

A Wesleyan church stood in South Street but was demolished in the late 1960s. John Wesley visited Dorking in January 1764 on one of many visits that he made to the town. Meetings were first held at the Red Lion Hotel until a meeting house was established in Church Street; it still stands in the car park of the King's Arms. The Baptist church is in regular use in Junction Road.

Below:

ST MARTIN'S CHURCH 1890 26762A

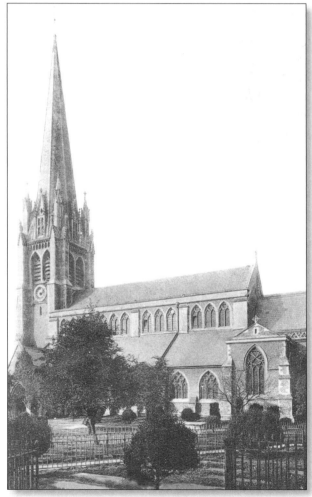

Other local churches, claimed to be 'old and steady', are Shere, Leigh, Mickleham, Abinger, Wotten and Betchworth: they have stood for centuries. St Barnabas's on Ranmore sits 700 feet above Dorking on Ranmore Common. Sir Gilbert Scott designed it in 1859 as the estate church for George Cubitt, the first Lord Ashcombe. In the churchyard lie the founder of Denbies Estate, and his three grandsons, Henry, Alick and William, who lost their lives in the First World War.

St Joseph's Catholic Church, designed by Frederick Arthur Walters, was erected in 1895 in Falkland Grove, off Coldharbour Lane (see 57647 pages 58-59). The site was donated by the Duke of Norfolk, who also contributed a substantial amount to the cost of

CHURCHES AND MEETING HOUSES

building the church. The church is a short distance from the Nower, another one of Dorking's parkland areas. The Barclay Family of Bury Hill gave the Nower to the people of Dorking on the celebration of Queen Victoria's Jubilee.

Many other denominations made their mark on Dorking. In 1672, following the Declaration of Indulgence, licences to preach in Dorking were issued to James Fisher and John Wood, who formed the Independent Congregational Church. A meeting house was established in West Street in 1719, which survived until 1834. The new building, which stands now, is the United Reformed Church; it has an attractive Italianate frontage, and was designed by the Dorking architect and builder, William Shearburn Senior.

The Friends Meeting House stands on Butter Hill in South Street, and below it is the beginning of the extensively-dug caves. The cave entrance can be seen in photograph 72900 on page 71: there is a gate in the metal railings in front of the bandstand to the left of the war memorial. Rumour has it that non-conformists used the caves to hold their meetings in private and solitude. The Quakers have played an active part in Dorking's community since the beginning of the 18th century.

Holy Trinity Church, Westcott was built between 1851-2 on land given by the Evelyn family, Lords of the Manor of Wotten. John Evelyn, the 17th-century diarist, was part of this noble family. With the expanding population of this small parish on the outskirts of Dorking, a church was needed for the local parishioners — in the 1851 census the count was 6,000. This church, another creation of Sir George Gilbert Scott, is in 14th-century Gothic style and mainly built of dressed flint with a shingled spire. It provided seating for about 250 people. The cost of the building was raised by subscription, and the principal benefactor was Mr Charles Barclay of Bury Hill. The living remained in the Barclay family until 1992, when it was transferred to the Bishop of Guildford.

COLDHARBOUR LANE 1907 57647

CHURCHES AND MEETING HOUSES

ST PAUL'S CHURCH 1903 50964

St Paul's Church was completed in 1857 as a second Anglican Church for the growing population of Dorking. Benjamin Ferry designed the church and the rectory (which sits next door).

WEST STREET

WEST STREET 1903 50957

WEST STREET

WEST STREET

Once the second trading area, West Street is now full of fine antique shops and small traders. The antique shops' trade is world-wide; they are visited by many collectors from Europe and the United States to purchase prized items.

West Street's other claim to fame is William Mullins, one of the Pilgrim Fathers, who lived here. The Mullins family established their home here in 1612 before venturing to Cape Cod on the 'Mayflower' in 1622. William and his brother John were wealthy cordwainers. Their house dates back to 1428, and is now an antique shop. The shop, once part of the Queen's Arms Inn, is said to be haunted: the ghost is of a young girl in a long flowing grey skirt, who gives a feeling of peace to those who see her. Often doors can be heard closing upstairs when no-one other than the owner is in the shop. Objects are also moved, and pictures taken down. There are several other ghosts in the Dorking area, including a headless horseman. Westcott Road (see 61411, right) lies to the end of West Street.

NELSON'S 'ENCYCLOPAEDIA', 1913

Dorking, a market town and parish of Surrey, England, west of Reigate. A church (1875) with spire of 210ft, commemorates Bishop Wilberforce; at Deepdene, in the immediate vicinity, Beaconsfield [Disraeli] wrote 'Coningsby' (published 1844). Dorking has trade of flour, corn, and lime and is noted for a breed of poultry. Pop. 7,700.

WEST STREET

Left:
WEST STREET 1922 72898

Below Left:
WESTCOTT ROAD 1909 61411

Below Right:
THE RECTORY, WESTCOTT ROAD 1905
53339

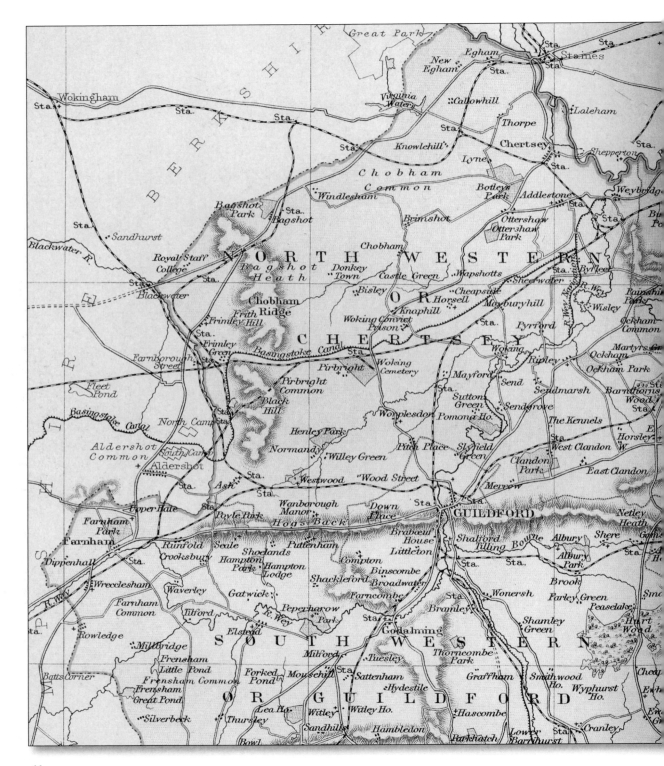

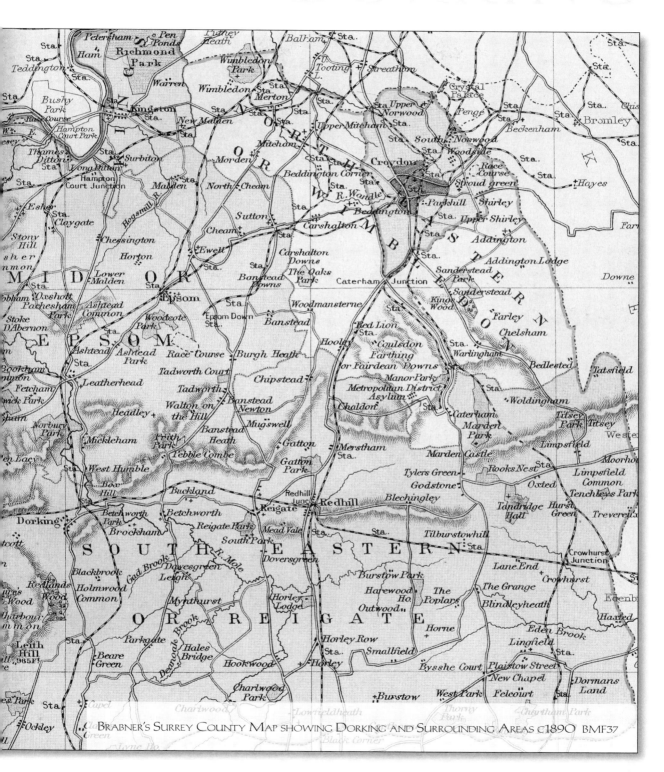

BRABNER'S SURREY COUNTY MAP showing DORKING and SURROUNDING AREAS c1890 BMF37

DORKING

SOUTH STREET AND PUMP CORNER 1906 55697

SOUTH STREET

This street forms the left fork of the junctions of the three main streets, and is the quietest of the three. On the corner stands the Bull's Head public house. Until just a few years ago the abattoir had its premises behind the pub, and here cattle were slaughtered on a regular basis. The White Lion stood exactly opposite until its demise. The Bull's Head is centre left and the White Lion is centre right in view 55697 on the previous page.

Shops and houses stood where now the bus stops are. On this site once stood the Old Bandstand, which commemorated the lives lost in 1914-18. The bandstand was removed in the early 1970s. The memorial to the dead of the First and Second World Wars also stands at this spot. Opposite is the Spotted Dog public house.

Further along South Street we find the Cricketers' Arms (last building on the right, 57641) and the Queen's Head (right, D45017) and the junction to Horsham Road and Vincent Lane. It was here that the old bus terminus stood until just a few years ago. Adjacent to Vincent Lane is Falkland Road. The Falkland Arms and the Prince of Wales both trade here. A few hundred yards along Horsham Road is the Bush Inn.

Top:
SOUTH STREET 1937 87852

Above:
THE WAR MEMORIAL 1922 72900

Right:
SOUTH STREET c1955 D45017

Opposite:
SOUTH STREET 1907 57641

THE VICTORIAN ERA

SOUTH STREET 1906 54661

The Stone Roof Cafe (left, on the bend) was the home of Colour Sergeant Frank Bourne, who took part in the battle of Rorke's Drift in 1879. Colour Sergeant Bourne was born on 27 April 1855. For his bravery in South Africa he was awarded the DCM and an annual annuity of £10. He was also awarded the OBE for his services to the Crown after serving forty-six years in the regiment of the 2nd/24th. Bourne retired to Dorking to live with his daughter, and died in Bromley aged ninety.

THE VICTORIAN ERA

In Victorian times Dorking was still a very rural town with a wide market place in the centre. The shops displayed their wares to the elements. The traffic was slower, but the pace was more fervent. The encouragement to buy was the most important thing of the day. At this time Dorking became a substantial trading town. There were the lime works, four working corn mills, the breweries, the cattle trade, a brick-works, and an iron foundry; Dorking also had its own water pumping station and gas and light works.

The train, the motorcar and the bicycle brought changes to Britain's way of life, and they brought many townspeople out to Dorking's countryside. There were several bicycle repair shops in the town. Mr Oliver West maintained and repaired bicycles in Dene Street (originally called Ram Alley), and C S Fuller had his business in South Street. Mr Fuller was also the first resident of Dorking to own a motorcar. Fuller's are still trading in bicycle repairs and sales, and they also trade in baby-wear, sports and fishing equipment — fishing licences can be purchased at Fuller's.

The Victorians brought enormous change to rural life and rural ways, but they also brought continuity as well. The role of the aristocracy and landed gentry remained crucial in rural affairs during the Victorian age. The British aristocracy was still predominantly country-based, and it was in their large country houses where they felt at home, and where most of their wealth and power was felt. There were many mansions in the Dorking area, but many are now lost, either through progress or just through the need for change.

Tea-rooms were plentiful. Loyns tea-rooms on Pump Corner was established in 1749 (right of 55697 on pages 68-69 - trading as T G Rix) and survived for about two hundred and twenty years. There was also the Stone Roof Café (on the left-hand side of the road just before it bends, 54661, on previous page).

Another tea-room in South Street was French's Tea Gardens, which adjoined the Stone Roof Café. The buildings have changed little over the last century. French's could accommodate quite a large number of clients; it catered especially for the cycling and touring clubs, and there were tables and seats in the garden at the back of the building.

HORSHAM ROAD 1905 53337

THE COTTAGE HOSPITAL 1906 54664

LOST MANSIONS

The lost mansion of Deepdene, owned by Lord Francis Hope, once stood near the busy A24. The Howard family first owned the estate as far back as the middle of the 17th century. Henry Frederick, Earl of Arundel, Surrey and Norfolk left his estate to his fourth son, Charles Howard of Greystoke, when he died in 1652. Charles Howard landscaped the gardens in Cromwell's time; they were laid out in the form of an amphitheatre, with a garden terrace and an open-air conservatory of flowers and rare plants, and were visited with admiration by John Evelyn, who declared that 'the site is worthy of Cowley's muse'. (Abraham Cowley was a distinguished poet during the Civil War era).

Thomas Hope (of the Hope Diamond fame), the son of a wealthy Amsterdam merchant, took possession of the mansion in 1808. He spared no expense in improving the structure, interior and grounds. In its later years, the house became a hotel, which was bought in 1939 by the Southern Railway Co. Although a Grade III listed building, it was demolished in 1969 to make way for offices and businesses.

Henry Talbot created Chart Park in 1746. (However, in 1694, the Hon Charles Howard, owner of the land at Deepdene, had originally planted seven acres of the south-facing slope of the area as a vineyard. At this time, Charles Howard had a house built at the base of the slope known as the Vineyard). Talbot was a merchant, who had become wealthy from several voyages to China with the East India Company. Talbot built a substantial house, and created a hanging garden on the side of a hill. The mansion was demolished, and the land was sold by Thomas Hope in 1814. Much of the land purchased by Talbot is now occupied by Dorking Golf Club; the golf course was built and landscaped in 1897. In the photograph of Chart Lane, the steps on the left lead to The Temple in the Deepdene estate.

DEEPDENE HOUSE 1891 29567

LOST MANSIONS

G PHILLIPS DEAN: 'TOURIST'S GUIDE TO THE COUNTY OF SURREY', 1887

'The great sight of Dorking is Deepdene ... one of the loveliest places in England, with a splendid art collection and charming grounds. The Dene (from which the house is named) is an exquisite glade at the back ...'

CHART LANE c1900 D45301

RAILWAYS

A proposed line from Redhill to Dorking was suggested in 1845. Parliamentary approval was given on 16 July 1846. At first it was suggested that the railway station should be built adjacent to St Martin's Church in 'The Lordship' (see picture 53332A on pages 48-49), now known as Meadow Bank Recreation Ground. By 1849 the railway was running a service from east to west, and Dorking Town station was the first to be built at the edge of the town. The line was principally built for freight traffic. The second station, built on the Leatherhead and Box Hill Road, opened in 1851, and was called Box Hill Station (see picture 57652 on page 25). The coming of the railways changed the townscape, and Dorking became a much busier town. The railway enabled the corn, lime and flour to be transported more easily, and the goods reached their destination more quickly and in a fresher condition.

There are now four railway stations; three are within ten minutes' walking distance from the town centre. Dorking's main station, once called Dorking North, is on the main line from Horsham to London's Victoria and Waterloo, which runs south to north on the outskirts of the town. The east to west line from Tunbridge Wells to Reading via Guildford is not electrified. This line crosses over the south to north line; the two stations which are served by this line are Dorking West (once called Dorking Town) and Deepdene, which was formerly Box Hill Station. This station is just five minutes' walk from the main line station. The fourth, already mentioned, is Boxhill & Westhumble.

THE STATION, SOUTH EASTERN RAILWAY 1888 21321

DORKING LIME

I t was said by many that 'Dorking lime is undoubtedly one of the finest quality of limestone in the county, if not England', and it was claimed that the chalk burnt into lime at Dorking was sought after by every mason and bricklayer in London. The West India and Wapping Docks were built with Dorking lime. In photograph 79501, right, we can see the white scar of the Brockham limeworks, worked at first by the Brockham Brick Company Ltd, and later by the Brockham Limes & Hearthstone Company Ltd. These works closed in 1925, and the land is managed by the Surrey Wildlife Trust as a nature reserve. Important lime kilns survive at the Betchworth and Brockham sites, and are in the process of being Scheduled as Ancient Monuments.

H. PIGOT & CO'S 'ROYAL NATIONAL DIRECTORY', 1839

'The town consists of one main street, with smaller ones diverging from it; being seated on the line of the road leading to Epsom, Worthing, Bognor and Brighton, it enjoyed a considerable thoroughfare. Exclusive of this local advantage, it possesses a good trade in corn, and upon the River Mole, which flows with rapidity, are several mills: there likewise is a great demand for Dorking lime, the limestone in this neighbourhood being considered superior to any other'.

THE REIGATE ROAD 1927 79501

THE DOWNS

The downs are mostly of chalk, and otherwise of sandstone, and each has its own special flora. The sandstone hills have their highest point in Leith Hill, 965ft above sea level, about five miles south-west of Dorking. From there they fall away in a picturesque series of steps, rising again to the same level as Leith Hill at Hindhead and Black Down. Leith Hill and its tower is a beauty spot not to be missed. With a good eye and on a clear day all the surrounding counties are visible. 'With the assistance of a telescope Windsor Castle, Frant Church, St Paul's Cathedral, Dunstable Downs, Ditchling Beacon and the spires and towers of forty-one churches can be seen.' (J S Bright, 1876). It has been said that a reflection of the sun on the sea has been noted. Richard Hull of Leith Hill Place built the tower in 1766 for his own delight, but also for that of his neighbours and everybody else. Richard was laid to rest beneath the tower, buried upside-down: he believed that the world would have turned on its axis before Judgement Day,

and he 'wished to stand before his Maker right way up'. This area is part of the National Trust's holdings; the estate now boasts over 900 acres owned by the Trust, and another 300 are under protection.

Box Hill has been called the most popular hill in the world, and Leith Hill most likely comes second. On each hill grow beeches, junipers, wild clematis and box, which delight the eye. The short, sweet, flower-starred turf is restful to the traveller. But there is a wilder, rugged air about Leith Hill and its approaches, which are clad in larch and fir and carpeted with scarlet and green whortleberry and purple heather. It has always been known as a rambler's paradise, for there are innumerable paths and bridleways that wind through the plantations and the heath.

The area covering Box Hill, the Holmwoods, Ranmore, Leith Hill and Coldharbour contain some of the finest woodland and natural habitats in Surrey. Generous donations of land and money by many public-spirited contributors over the years have helped to ensure the upkeep of this fine and beautiful area.

A VIEW FROM THE NOWER 1936 87311

CAPE PLACE 1913   65212

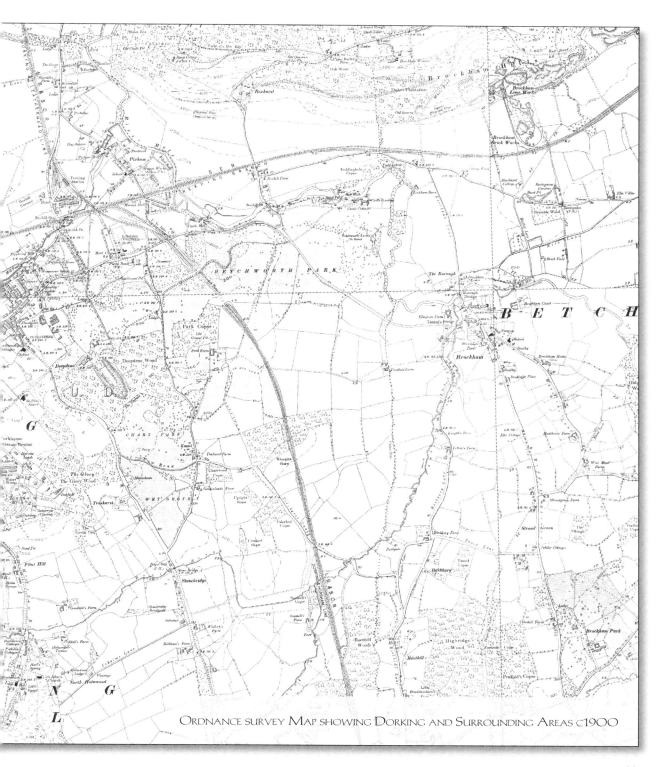

ORDNANCE SURVEY MAP SHOWING DORKING AND SURROUNDING AREAS c1900

Names of Pre-Publication Buyers

FRANCIS FRITH'S
TOWN & CITY
MEMORIES

The following people have kindly supported this book by purchasing limited edition copies prior to publication.

Surrey Advertiser

Annie Anderson, 'Always in our thoughts'

For Father's Day, Geoff Banwell, love Rachel & Tony

In memory of The Bennett & Skilton Families from Dorking

H Blight

The Brewer Family

John, Nancy & Paul Browne

John & Margaret Browning

Christine Burden

To the best Mum & Dad in the world, June & Dave Burden

In memory of Dorothy & Jack Chatfield of Dorking

The Chatfield Family

Wilfrid & Judith Dawkins

Happy 70th Dorothy love John x

In memory of Shaun P Flavell

Sheila Ford

The Fountain Family

Terry & June Fowler

Mr & Mrs B Fry & Family, Dorking

Grace Scott (nee Spence)

In memory of John A Hall

Brenda Hinds

To all the grandchildren love Gran & Grandad, K & B Hoskins

Peter James

Laurie, Lou & Bridger Jenkins

P H Keller

Peter & Marion Knowles

Michael & Olive Longhurst

K & S Lowe

Leslie & Edward Munn

In memory of Grandfather and Father who owned Munns Stores, Lyons Court

All the Nash Family at Rose Hill Lodge

Gill & Phil Perkins

Rosie & Tom Peters

Mrs Jacqueline Peters

To Maureen Potter from her son Jack

Nicola, Trevor & Annabel Prout

Jean Ridley, In loving memory of Thomas

To Pete & Michelle Scott from Mary & Mark

The Sellers Family

Mr & Mrs S L Smith

Pauline Spong

Alice Stubbs

John Tucker

Mr P Warrington

In memory of Miss E L Weller, the custodian of Leith Hill Tower for 60 years

Robert George West, Dorking

Elaine Wilson

As a tribute to my loving parents, Patricia Worden

To Mr & Mrs Young from all the family

INDEX

The Francis Frith Collection Titles

www.francisfrith.co.uk

The Francis Frith Collection publishes over 100 new titles each year. A selection of those currently available is listed below. For latest catalogue please contact The Francis Frith Collection. **Town Books** 96 pages, approximately 75 photos. **County and Themed Books** 128 pages, approximately 135 photos (unless specified). All titles hardback with laminated case and jacket, except those indicated pb (paperback)

Available from your local bookshop or from the publisher

The Francis Frith Collection Titles (continued)

Lancaster, Morecombe and Heysham Pocket Album
Leeds PA
Leicester
Leicestershire
Lincolnshire Living Memoires
Lincolnshire Pocket Album
Liverpool and Merseyside
London PA
Ludlow
Maidenhead
Maidstone
Malmesbury
Manchester PA
Marlborough
Matlock
Merseyside Living Memories
Nantwich and Crewe
New Forest
Newbury Living Memories
Newquay to St Ives
North Devon Living Memories
North London
North Wales
North Yorkshire
Northamptonshire
Northumberland
Northwich
Nottingham
Nottinghamshire PA
Oakham
Odiham Then and Now
Oxford Pocket Album
Oxfordshire
Padstow
Pembrokeshire
Penzance
Petersfield Then and Now
Plymouth
Poole and Sandbanks
Preston PA
Ramsgate Old and New
Reading Pocket Album
Redditch Living Memories
Redhill to Reigate
Rhondda Valley Living Mems
Richmond
Ringwood
Rochdale
Romford PA
Salisbury PA
Scotland
Scottish Castles
Sevenoaks and Tonbridge
Sheffield and South Yorkshire PA
Shropshire
Somerset
South Devon Coast
South Devon Living Memories
South East London
Southampton PA
Southend PA

Southport
Southwold to Aldeburgh
Stourbridge Living Memories
Stratford upon Avon
Stroud
Suffolk
Suffolk PA
Surrey Living Memories
Sussex
Sutton
Swanage and Purbeck
Swansea Pocket Album
Swindon Living Memories
Taunton
Teignmouth
Tenby and Saundersfoot
Tiverton
Torbay
Truro
Uppingham
Villages of Kent
Villages of Surrey
Villages of Sussex PA
Wakefield and the Five Towns Living Memories
Warrington
Warwick
Warwickshire PA
Wellingborough Living Memories
Wells
Welsh Castles
West Midlands PA
West Wiltshire Towns
West Yorkshire
Weston-super-Mare
Weymouth
Widnes and Runcorn
Wiltshire Churches
Wiltshire Living memories
Wiltshire PA
Wimborne
Winchester PA
Windermere
Windsor
Wirral
Wokingham and Bracknell
Woodbridge
Worcester
Worcestershire
Worcestershire Living Memories
Wyre Forest
York PA
Yorkshire
Yorkshire Coastal Memories
Yorkshire Dales
Yorkshire Revisited

See Frith books on the internet at www.francisfrith.co.uk

FRITH PRODUCTS & SERVICES

Francis Frith would doubtless be pleased to know that the pioneering publishing venture he started in 1860 still continues today. Over a hundred and forty years later, The Francis Frith Collection continues in the same innovative tradition and is now one of the foremost publishers of vintage photographs in the world. Some of the current activities include:

Interior Decoration

Today Frith's photographs can be seen framed and as giant wall murals in thousands of pubs, restaurants, hotels, banks, retail stores and other public buildings throughout the country. In every case they enhance the unique local atmosphere of the places they depict and provide reminders of gentler days in an increasingly busy and frenetic world.

Product Promotions

Frith products are used by many major companies to promote the sales of their own products or to reinforce their own history and heritage. Frith promotions have been used by Hovis bread, Courage beers, Scots Porage Oats, Colman's mustard, Cadbury's foods, Mellow Birds coffee, Dunhill pipe tobacco, Guinness, and Bulmer's Cider.

Genealogy and Family History

As the interest in family history and roots grows world-wide, more and more people are turning to Frith's photographs of Great Britain for images of the towns, villages and streets where their ancestors lived; and, of course, photographs of the churches and chapels where their ancestors were christened, married and buried are an essential part of every genealogy tree and family album.

Frith Products

All Frith photographs are available Framed or just as Mounted Prints and Posters (size 23 x 16 inches). These may be ordered from the address below. From time to time other products - Address Books, Calendars, Table Mats, etc - are available.

The Internet

Already ninety thousand Frith photographs can be viewed and purchased on the internet through the Frith websites and a myriad of partner sites.

For more detailed information on Frith companies and products, look at these sites:

www.francisfrith.co.uk
www.francisfrith.com
(for North American visitors)

See the complete list of Frith Books at:

www.francisfrith.co.uk

This web site is regularly updated with the latest list of publications from The Francis Frith Collection. If you wish to buy books relating to another part of the country that your local bookshop does not stock, you may purchase on-line.

For further information, trade, or author enquiries please contact us at the address below:
The Francis Frith Collection, Frith's Barn, Teffont, Salisbury, Wiltshire, England SP3 5QP.
Tel: +44 (0)1722 716 376 Fax: +44 (0)1722 716 881 Email: sales@francisfrith.co.uk

See Frith books on the internet at www.francisfrith.co.uk

FREE PRINT OF YOUR CHOICE

Mounted Print
Overall size 14 x 11 inches (355 x 280mm)

Choose any Frith photograph in this book.
Simply complete the Voucher opposite and return it with your remittance for £2.25 (to cover postage and handling) and we will print the photograph of your choice in SEPIA (size 11 x 8 inches) and supply it in a cream mount with a burgundy rule line (overall size 14 x 11 inches).
Please note: photographs with a reference number starting with a "Z" are not Frith photographs and cannot be supplied under this offer.
Offer valid for delivery to one UK address only.

PLUS: **Order additional Mounted Prints at HALF PRICE - £7.49 each** (normally £14.99)
If you would like to order more Frith prints from this book, possibly as gifts for friends and family, you can buy them at half price (with no additional postage and handling costs).

PLUS: **Have your Mounted Prints framed**
For an extra £14.95 per print you can have your mounted print(s) framed in an elegant polished wood and gilt moulding, overall size 16 x 13 inches (no additional postage and handling required).

IMPORTANT!

These special prices are only available if you use this form to order . You must use the ORIGINAL VOUCHER on this page (no copies permitted). We can only despatch to one UK address. This offer cannot be combined with any other offer.

Send completed Voucher form to:
The Francis Frith Collection, Frith's Barn, Teffont, Salisbury, Wiltshire SP3 5QP

CHOOSE A PHOTOGRAPH FROM THIS BOOK

Voucher for **FREE** *and Reduced Price Frith Prints*

Please do not photocopy this voucher. Only the original is valid, so please fill it in, cut it out and return it to us with your order.

Picture ref no	Page no	Qty	Mounted @ £7.49	Framed + £14.95	Total Cost £
		1	Free of charge*	£	£
			£7.49	£	£
			£7.49	£	£
			£7.49	£	£
			£7.49	£	£
			£7.49	£	£

Please allow 28 days for delivery.
Offer available to one UK address only

* Post & handling	£2.25
Total Order Cost	£

Title of this book . . . .

I enclose a cheque/postal order for £ . . . . made payable to 'The Francis Frith Collection'

OR please debit my Mastercard / Visa / Maestro / Amex card, details below

Card Number

Issue No (Maestro only)   Valid from (Maestro)

Expires   Signature

Name Mr/Mrs/Ms . . . .
Address . . . .
. . . .
. . . .
. . . . Postcode . . . .
Daytime Tel No . . . .
Email . . . .

ISBN: 1-85937-960-5   Valid to 31/12/07

Would you like to find out more about Francis Frith?

We have recently recruited some entertaining speakers who are happy to visit local groups, clubs and societies to give an illustrated talk documenting Frith's travels and photographs. If you are a member of such a group and are interested in hosting a presentation, we would love to hear from you.

Our speakers bring with them a small selection of our local town and county books, together with sample prints. They are happy to take orders. A small proportion of the order value is donated to the group who have hosted the presentation. The talks are therefore an excellent way of fundraising for small groups and societies.

Can you help us with information about any of the Frith photographs in this book?

We are gradually compiling an historical record for each of the photographs in the Frith archive. It is always fascinating to find out the names of the people shown in the pictures, as well as insights into the shops, buildings and other features depicted.

If you recognize anyone in the photographs in this book, or if you have information not already included in the author's caption, do let us know. We would love to hear from you, and will try to publish it in future books or articles.

Our production team

Frith books are produced by a small dedicated team at offices in the converted Grade II listed 18th-century barn at Teffont near Salisbury, illustrated above. Most have worked with the Frith Collection for many years. All have in common one quality: they have a passion for the Frith Collection. The team is constantly expanding, but currently includes:

Paul Baron, Phillip Brennan, Jason Buck, John Buck, Ruth Butler, Heather Crisp, David Davies, Louis du Mont, Isobel Hall, Lucy Hart, Julian Hight, Peter Horne, James Kinnear, Karen Kinnear, Tina Leary, Stuart Login, David Marsh, Lesley-Ann Millard, Sue Molloy, Glenda Morgan, Wayne Morgan, Sarah Roberts, Kate Rotondetto, Dean Scource, Eliza Sackett, Terence Sackett, Sandra Sampson, Adrian Sanders, Sandra Sanger, Julia Skinner, Miles Smith, Lewis Taylor, Shelley Tolcher, Lorraine Tuck, David Turner, Amanita Wainwright and Ricky Williams.